CO-PARENTING

A B C s

Effective tips from a **divorced**
divorce lawyer and parent

CO-PARENTING
ABCs

Effective tips from a **divorced**
divorce lawyer and parent

Allison Schreiber Lee

Co-Parenting ABCs
Effective tips from a divorced divorce lawyer and parent
Copyright © 2021 Allison Schreiber Lee

Paperback ISBN: 978-1-7368317-0-0
E-Book ISBN: 978-1-7368317-1-7

Library of Congress Control Number: 2021908771

Edited by: Lila Stromer Editorial Services
Cover and interior design: Peggy Nehmen, n-kcreative.com

Printed in the United States of America
First Printing 2021

Published by: ABC by Allison, LLC, St. Louis Missouri
https://allison-thisisthelife.blogspot.com

**To M and D, who make
me a better parent.**

**To R and D, who make
me a better co-parent.**

Contents

Introduction

What is co-parenting?

In my practice as a divorce lawyer, I think of co-parenting as "cooperative parenting." It's parenting with someone with whom you are no longer in a relationship, yet you must remain connected because you have a child to raise. It's making decisions as parents together even though you are no longer together as a family. This includes everything from selecting classes (and signing off for anything that requires a permission slip), to getting medical care, choosing extracurricular activities, and getting a driver's license (and this is clearly only a fraction of the list.) Maintaining a functional co-parenting relationship is essential for raising your child into adulthood. Research indicates that children do better when parents can cooperate on behalf of their child and minimize conflict. (*American Academy of Child and Adolescent Psychiatry*, Jan. 2017).

What is this book?

It is a quick and easy reference guide for co-parents to work together constructively to raise a child when they no longer share a romantic relationship or a home. It gives tools, tricks, insights, and advice about what a good co-parenting relationship is and what minefields and pitfalls to avoid. It is not long or involved, but it offers a way for you to check in and give yourself the best opportunity to help the one person that co-parenting is about: your child. This is a book for parents who are court-ordered to parent a child together and/or those who believe the basic tenet that all children are always better with both parents in their lives. The information is laid out to help you quickly find what you need when you need it, or you can read it from start to finish for an overall perspective.

The examples are designed to show how a parental relationship can go off track, how to prevent that from happening, and, more importantly, how to recover when it does. They offer guidance on how to move forward in a new life while you have parenting responsibilities with your ex. They include examples for when you receive unwanted advice from loved ones and friends; when one of you starts a new relationship, bringing a new person into the mix; what to do when life events conflict or require you to be in attendance together; and so many others. As a divorce lawyer, I have guided divorced parents; as a divorced co-parent, I have lived the lessons newly divorced parents are just learning. For consistency throughout the examples, I refer to the imaginary parents as "Mom" and "Dad" and my imaginary child is named "Jake," but this book is designed for divorced parents of all genders and orientations, with children of all genders and orientations, looking to raise a happier child.

Finally, if you are in an abusive relationship, that situation is outside the scope of this book. Please check with a mental health provider before using the tools in this book because co-parenting with an abusive parent can lead to further instances of psychological and emotional abuse for you and your child.

So, who am I to write this book?

Let me start with what I am not. I am not a therapist or a psychologist or a behavioral scientist. I have not done any studies on co-parenting.

But I'm very experienced with this subject because I've been a divorced mom for over 15 years. My children were very young when I got divorced from their father, so I have personally been through many phases and stages of co-parenting.

I am also a divorce attorney. I have counseled (in the legal sense) countless parents going through very contentious divorces and parenting proceedings. I have advised many parents on what to say and, more importantly, what not to say to each other and to their children.

To paraphrase Julius Caesar, experience is the greatest teacher of all. I have it in spades when it comes to co-parenting with an ex, personally and professionally.

I hope this guide is useful to you. Most of all, I hope it is helpful for your children.

Disclaimer

This book is not intended as legal advice and should not be taken as such. Laws in every county in each U.S. state and in every country are different. This book is only intended to give practical guidance based on practical experience, for how to co-parent effectively when you are no longer together as a family unit. If you have any legal questions about parenting, you should contact an experienced family law attorney in your area.

The examples in this book are not reflective of any particular circumstance that I have encountered as a divorced parent or divorce attorney. They are provided for illustrative purposes only.

A.

Always

Always be courteous. Remember this, even when you don't want to be. Even when the other person doesn't deserve it. Even when your co-parent is being discourteous to you. Your children are watching what you do and how you react. Your behavior, whether you realize it or not, impacts their relationship with you and with your ex. A parent who is sad and scared can mean the child becomes sad and scared, too. Having a parent who is angry and bitter teaches a child to react with anger and bitterness. When you are courteous to your co-parent, it shows your child that you can be on the same team, even though you are not together anymore. It allows your child to be happy at both houses, feeling secure and comforted that the end of your relationship together, does not mean disaster for the child's relationship with both of you. Your child will grow up knowing that people can end a relationship with maturity.

Courtesy does not mean, however, that you have no backbone or that you don't stand up for yourself. It does mean that when you disagree with your co-parent, you do so respectfully, calmly, and unemotionally. If you disagree with a parent at your child's school, would you yell at them publicly or send a text or email calling them names? If you stop to think of your co-parent as someone with whom you are friendly—but not friends—and

5

with whom you have to work together even if you don't like each other, your tone will change, your word choice will be different, and your whole approach to them will transform. Take time to gather your thoughts and remove the emotion from your response.

Examples

Just a month after the divorce is final, Dad picks up Jake at Mom's house, but with his new girlfriend in the car. She was an issue in the marriage, and her presence is hurtful to Mom. After they leave, Mom grabs her phone to text Dad how inconsiderate he is.

When Jake is with Dad, Mom calls several times a day. She often calls first thing in the morning and last thing right before bed. Dad finds Mom's contact intrusive, especially because he is trying to get Jake used to his new house. Dad is about to email Mom with some less-than-kind words about always butting into his routine with Jake.

In the first example, things would have been better had Mom taken a pause to call a friend to talk through her emotions (although please note "Discretion" below). She waits to text her ex when she's not so upset and can articulate her feelings: "When you bring your girlfriend to get Jake, it brings up a lot of difficult emotions for me. I'm sure your relationship is important to you, but could you let me know ahead of time that she will be there so I'm not surprised? I would really appreciate it. Thanks."

In the second example, Dad walks away from his computer to gather his thoughts before typing something he can't take back. He instead writes: "I know the time away from Jake can be difficult; I feel that way too, but as you know, getting out the door in the mornings can be hectic. I am wondering if we can set a time each evening for you to talk to him, either before or right after dinner. Thanks."

By keeping your tone and wording neutral and respectful, you allow your co-parent to respond in kind, keeping the relationship moving forward in a more positive and productive manner.

B.

Business

The general rule is to mind your own. What goes on at the other parent's house is none of your business unless it objectively puts your child in harm's way. Things at your ex's house will not be the same as at your house. You may eat different foods or have different ways of celebrating holidays, but two households means children get to experience variety in their lives. Mothers and fathers may not parent in similar ways, even when they live in the same house. Diverse traditions and experiences at different houses are not bad for a child—they're actually healthy. Encouraging your child to enjoy being at both houses helps your child feel more settled and comfortable in each home. This is powerful for a child's well-being.

Examples

Jake mentions to Dad that he got to sleep over at a new friend's house when he was with Mom, and he had a great time. Dad doesn't know the new friend, and Mom didn't say anything about a sleepover. Dad starts asking questions about the new friend: where did they meet, how long have they known each other, did Mom meet the parents before Jake slept over, etc. Jake can tell Dad is upset but also feels disloyal to Mom if he says too much.

When Jake's parents got divorced, Mom wasn't working. She had been a stay-at-home parent for 10 years—since Jake was born—which was a factor in determining spousal and child support issues during the divorce. It is now a year after the divorce, and Jake is talking to Dad about his winter class party and how Mom is in charge of the snacks. Dad asks Jake how often Mom comes to his school for lunch and if Mom is working at all. The questions make Jake feel terrible about having brought up the party, which he had been excited about. He also doesn't know the answers to Dad's questions, so he also feels small and stupid.

It wasn't fair of the parents to question Jake because it put him in the middle, which is exactly where he doesn't belong. If you have questions about what is happening at the other parent's house, seek the information from the other parent directly. It protects your child, prevents you from making assumptions, and forces you to have a working relationship with your ex.

C.

Compassion

It is certainly difficult to be compassionate toward someone who caused you pain or treated you badly, but getting to that place with your co-parent is a game changer. As the saying goes, there are three sides to every story—yours, mine, and the truth—and each person has a different perception of events. You may never come to see your ex's side of the story, and that doesn't matter. What matters is that you have a child together. Your relationship is now only about your child's life. You will eventually ask your ex for something, or vice versa. Before you leap to conclusions, or react without complete information about a situation, take a breath and have a conversation. Ask why they are making the request, what the concerns are, and how they propose to solve the issue. Talking through an issue rather than leaping to a conclusion without all the facts can change the course of the response. Learning how to have conversations about your child, without making assumptions about the other parent, will have a significant long-term effect on your parenting relationship.

Examples

Mom asks Dad if Jake can stay with her for a few extra days because he has the flu. Dad is livid. It's his time with Jake and he is perfectly capable of taking care of Jake.

11

Dad asks if he can have some additional days so Jake can spend time with his grandmother. Mom is annoyed because she'll lose some of her designated time with Jake.

If either parent had first asked why a few extra days were needed, the initial angry responses would have been avoided. Dad would learn that Mom's father had the flu so severely that he had to be hospitalized, and Jake has a worse-than-normal flu too. It seems best to not shuffle him around right now but to just let him get better. And if Mom had known that her ex-mother-in-law was dying, she might have been more understanding.

If both conversations had been complete, not just a request and an immediate response, they would each learned that the other parent was willing to make up the time missed after the immediate situation ended. Of course, if both parents had been more specific and forthcoming in their requests, they could have avoided the initial misunderstanding. It takes both parents to give enough information and both to ask complete questions before reacting.

Especially in the case with his grandmother, Jake will see his parents work together through difficult and sad situations, putting their differences aside for the benefit of other family members. This is a teachable moment for Jake and a co-parenting success for Mom and Dad.

D.

Discretion

As tempting as it is, don't tell everyone you know about your issues with your ex. Do you *need* to share that you are fighting over summer camp or getting a driver's license? Bad-mouthing your ex to people in your child's life hurts your child, making things like attending a joint sporting event or combined-family event unnecessarily uncomfortable. Of course, you may have a good friend to confide in, but both parents need to be discreet about when and to whom they talk about their ex. Airing your dirty laundry to a large number of people will only backfire at some point and prevent you from keeping your child out of family disputes.

Examples

Grandma calls to see if Mom is getting the child support money from her ex. Jake's parents have recently come to an agreement that Jake can stay with Mom more days in exchange for Dad paying less in child support. Mom had discussed this with her attorney, and she is comfortable with this agreement because it means Jake is with her more often during the week, giving her more opportunities to help with homework and be with him in the mornings. Grandma only asks about finances because she is still mad at Dad for the divorce, and she doesn't understand this arrangement is much preferred by her daughter.

One of the other dads at Jake's baseball practice, approaches Dad about the divorce. In attempting to be supportive, he says, "If you ever want to talk about what caused the split, just let me know. I know how hard it is when it's not your fault."

In the first case, Mom should say to her mother, "We are working it all out. I'm comfortable with where things are, and I know that Jake is in a good place with both of us. I appreciate your concern, but I really don't want to discuss the specifics."

In the second case, Dad should tell his friend, "I appreciate your support. I have a good attorney and she is helping me through the legal part of it. Right now, I'm just focused on Jake and trying to help him through this transition."

In both scenarios, the grandmother and the friend are trying to be helpful, but the parents oversharing will not serve Jake's overall interest. Family talks to other family members, friends talk to other friends, and soon your personal life becomes fodder for gossip and speculation. That is not good for you, your child, or your co-parent. It is natural to want to discuss things with friends and family, but discretion will better serve you and your child in the long run.

E.

Energy

Let's talk about misplaced energy. When you and your ex disagree, take stock if you are fighting simply to prove the other parent wrong. If so, that's misplaced energy. Is it worth your energy to argue about which of Jake's items get to stay at whose house? Is it worth the energy to badmouth your ex, not realizing it makes your child not want to be open with you about his feelings? Are you expending energy just to be right or prove a point, or are you expending energy because the answer will benefit your child? You now have a new life of your own: use your energy to make it the best it can be instead of wasting it on useless arguments with your ex. Co-parenting should only be about what is best for your child. Your energy should be directed toward what will help your child, and not what will hurt your ex.

Examples
Both parents moved to new locations after the divorce, so they each now live closer to work. Mom's apartment has a pool and Dad's house has a large backyard. Mom constantly grumbles that Dad spent too much money on his house, and Dad complains about how far Mom has moved away from Jake's school. Jake, who is the only one who matters, is content at both places, but he feels disloyal if he tells

Dad he likes Mom's pool and other amenities and if he tells Mom he loves running around the backyard.

Dad bought Jake a new fishing vest so they can go fishing together on weekends. Mom has a lake near her house, and Jake wants to show Mom what he has learned about fishing from Dad. At first, Dad is reluctant to let Jake bring the fishing vest to Mom's because he is the one who bought it, and in the past Mom told Jake that certain items she bought for him must stay at her house. So, why shouldn't the vest stay at his house?

In the first instance, both parents would be better off being supportive of the new places they have each moved into. Making negative comments or putting the other parent down is bad for Jake. If instead, they spent their energy making Jake feel comfortable in both locations, his transition from living under one roof to under two would easier for him.

In the second instance, Dad needs to realize that the vest is actually Jake's. He bought it, but he gave it to Jake. And if he wants Jake to really use it and appreciate what he's learned about fishing, letting him travel with the vest becomes about Jake fishing anywhere and not about the item itself. It may make Mom realize that allowing Jake to bring belongings back and forth would help Jake feel more settled in both locations, which is essential during this transition period.

F.

Forgiveness

Let go of past hurts. This is where a good therapist comes in. Not your best friend, but a professional. A best friend is going to take your side and defend you, no matter what; that's why they are your best friend. What you need is a therapist to give you the tools and teach you how to process the past and move more effectively into the future. Forgiveness allows you the space to redefine your relationship with your ex. With the help of a therapist, you learn how to change the paradigm you have with your ex. Additionally, if you understand your role in the divorce, you hopefully won't repeat the same mistakes with someone new. Co-parenting necessitates good communication with your ex, which is impossible if you are still reliving past emotional injuries.

Remember that your children are now the focus of this relationship, not what your ex did or didn't do. And like it or not, you are in each other's lives, at least until your children are adults. When you focus on your children, forgiveness comes more easily and decisions become easier to make. It's not about the hurts that either of you may be carrying, but what would make your children more fulfilled and well-rounded. Keeping your children in the forefront of your mind as you move forward in your new relationship with your ex, allows you to provide the best life possible in circumstances they had no hand in creating.

Examples

Dad had a girlfriend at the end of his marriage to Mom. He has now remarried and is expecting a child with his new wife. Jake is excited to be a big brother but knows that this news makes Mom sad. He feels the need to protect his mother, so he doesn't talk with her about it, even though he really wants to.

Mom suffered from depression during the marriage. Through the help of a psychiatrist, medication, and intensive therapy, her depression is well controlled and she is stable and healthy. Dad still worries about Jake being at Mom's house. He constantly asks Jake: Is there food in the house? Is the house clean? Is the laundry done? While his concerns are understandable, Jake knows that Mom is different than she used to be, and they talk openly and honestly about her past and present. He feels very connected to Mom and is proud of her for how far she's come.

In relation to her ex moving on and Jake becoming a big brother, if Mom were to change her focus from how she feels about her ex's new life, to focusing on Jake's excitement, she would allow Jake to talk to her about it. They could buy a gift from him for the new baby, and talk about him being an older sibling at Dad's and an only child at Mom's. Setting aside her feelings will allow Jake to embrace this new situation, and also strengthen Mom's relationship with Jake.

If Dad were to ask questions with an open mind rather than anticipating the worst, he would hear about how far Jake's relationship with his mother has come and how much healthier Mom is as a person and a parent. Instead of making Jake feel defensive and scared, Dad's relationship with Jake would likely grow stronger because Jake wouldn't be nervous about answering questions regarding what happens while he's at his mother's house.

G.

Golden

Remember the Golden Rule and treat your co-parent as you would like to be treated. A simple change in language can change the course of a conversation, an interaction, and even your co-parenting relationship. Asking, "Do you think Jake would like to play soccer? What do you think if we signed him up? Would you be okay paying for half the costs?" is much more likely to be well-received than "I'm going to sign Jake up for soccer. Let me know if you will agree to pay your half." The first is an invitation to discuss an activity and how to pay for it. The second is a declaration, with the assumption that the other parent will try to shirk their financial responsibility. Remember, if someone with whom you already have a difficult relationship is negative in their requests, you may be more likely to say no automatically. But if you and your ex remember the Golden Rule and *ask* for opinions, you open up a dialogue and are more apt to be engaged, to listen, and to consider to the suggestion.

Examples

Dad's extended family is planning a cruise during the summer, which occurs over some of Mom's time with Jake. Dad offers Mom seven days in a row when they get back from the trip, so she doesn't lose any time with Jake. Dad tells Mom that the cruise will include Jake's grandparents, aunts, uncles, and cousins from around the country. Mom has no plans, yet she's annoyed by the switch in scheduling.

Mom wants to sign Jake up for soccer with his friends in the neighborhood, but the practices will occur during the times he is with both parents. Dad would prefer to spend time hanging out with Jake at his house rather than taking him to soccer at least once a week. But he also knows that Jake has been talking about the soccer team with other kids from the neighborhood and is excited about the prospect of playing.

With regards to the cruise, Mom is focusing on her needs and wanting to keep the agreed-upon schedule as is. If she instead focused on Jake making memories with his other family, her decision is easy. She would allow Jake to go on the family trip in exchange for a full week with him. Dad isn't cutting her time short; he is only asking for a change for a special event.

As with the cruise, Dad needs to think about what Jake wants, taking himself out of the picture. He could see that letting him play soccer is the better choice than saying no. While spending time with him at home is certainly important, so is allowing Jake the freedom to socialize and play a game he clearly enjoys.

Focusing on your child is not as easy when it comes to perceived issues of safety. What if your ex wants to sign your child up for football (at the child's request), but you are worried about the danger involved? What if you want to let your child visit your family across country traveling alone (taking all the necessary precautions with the airline), but your ex is worried that your child isn't ready to take a flight alone. In those cases, it would be best for you both to talk to each other directly about your concerns or get input from a neutral third party, such as the football coach or an airline representative. Is the football no-contact? Is there another sport your child likes that both parents can agree on? Would it be preferred if one parent take your child on the trip to visit family, if time off from work can be arranged? There's often no right or wrong answer to more difficult questions like these, but communication leads to understanding. With communication, neither of you is defending your position or making assumptions. Talking to each other can lead to outcomes that are agreeable to both parties. It is easier to say yes to someone who has been kind and it's more likely you'll both be receptive if you've shown each other consideration in the past.

H.

Honor

Honor the positive impact the other parent has on your child. Children know that they are influenced by both of their parents. There are aspects of their talent and personalities that reflect each of their parents. Helping a child appreciate the influence the other parent has on them, and nurturing that in your child, allows the child to feel supported and loved. Bad-mouthing the other parent can also make the child feel less worthy. If a child hears, "Your mom is so lazy, why doesn't she get a job?" or "Your dad doesn't care about anyone but himself," they internalize these comments and feel bad about themselves when they do the same. If a child hears "You are so good at math, just like your mom!" or "I love how you can draw so well. You definitely get that from your dad!", the child will beam with pride and will see that parents who are no longer together can still see the good in the other, and in the child.

Examples

Dad is frustrated by the amount of child support he pays. After Mom reaches about sharing the expense of buying new cleats for Jake, Dad asks, "What does your Mom do with the child support I give her?

She's always been terrible with money. Maybe you should ask her to use some of the money I send her to buy your cleats."

Mom asks Jake about his skinned knees after coming back from Dad's. Jake says his father was teaching him to rollerblade and he fell a few times. Mom says in exasperation, "Doesn't your dad know that's not safe? Why is he trying to teach you how to rollerblade at your age?" Now Jake feels clumsy and embarrassed by an activity that originally brought him a lot of joy.

In the first example, Dad should check with his attorney to ensure the amount of child support he is paying is correct and confirm the division of expenses. Assuming both of those items are in line, Dad should realize that venting his frustration only makes it harder on Jake. If Jake needs or wants something else, like a new pair of sneakers, he may connect it with what Dad said about money and feel too ashamed or worried to ask either parent for them.

In the second example, Mom took her worries about rollerblading directly to Jake, which may shut him down and prevent him either from doing an activity he enjoys with his father or hiding it from his mother. A better reaction would be to reach out to Dad directly about her concerns, and perhaps ask that he buy protective equipment, such as knee pads.

I.

Important

Decide what's important and forget the rest. Don't fight about who is buying school supplies; just talk about who wants to do it and who has the time to do it, and let that person do the shopping. If it is important to each of you, alternate every other year. When faced with a potential argument, take a breath to decide if the subject is important enough to pick a fight. If so, still engage in a respectful manner. Don't point fingers or make accusations. If you can't reach a mutual decision, is there a neutral third party, such as a pediatrician or school counselor, you can both consult for input? If not, or if the disagreement persists after the consultation, take a break from the subject. Tell your co-parent you need to cool off and you'll make arrangements to talk when you're ready (and then keep that promise). If it is still important after taking a break, you may want to consider emailing instead of talking on the phone, since the former allows you time to think before pushing "send" and the latter may escalate things too quickly. Texting is often a bad idea when hashing out an argument because it is too easy to type and send something you'll regret later. It is possible to debate about important issues effectively, but there needs to be space between responses. And there's also great benefit to allowing something that isn't important to fall by the wayside.

Examples

Mom wants to take a trip out of town with Jake, who's in first grade. Mom would rather drive than fly, but that means Jake will miss one day of school after a holiday weekend. Dad can't afford to take Jake on any trips, so he wants to say no.

Dad is having a hard time with Jake and wants to go to counseling with him. He reaches out to Mom, and they agree that a counselor could help Dad and Jake work out their relationship. The scheduled appointments are one day a week for 12 weeks, but it is on one of Mom's days. Mom recognizes that Dad and Jake are having problems, but why should this cause her to reschedule her time for 12 weeks?

Dad's decision-making would be helped if he thought through why this request bothers him and why he wants to say no. When he realizes that it's about his own feelings about money, and he takes himself out of the equation, then the question becomes: How important is it that Jake is missing one day of school in first grade? The answer is not very important at this age.

Mom understands that Dad and Jake need to learn how to talk to each other productively. Their relationship was never great, so it's important to reinforce that Dad asking for help is a good thing. Taking all of that into account, Mom rescheduling one day a week for 12 weeks is less important than Dad working on his relationship with Jake.

J.

Judgment

It's easy to judge someone from afar, especially an ex. When they leave, you feel betrayed. When you leave, you feel resentful. When you look at the other person's new life, your view is distorted by the lens of the old relationship. In fact, however, no one can never know what's going on in someone else's mind or house without talking to them. A great deal of co-parenting miscommunication comes from making assumptions and then judging the other person based on how you feel. But often those judgments and assumptions turn out to be untrue. Ask questions and really listen to the answers before you make up your mind about a situation. These difficult yet simple acts can help soften the hard lines we've drawn, leading divorced people to be better co-parents.

Examples

Mom wants Jake to attend private school. Dad wants Jake to attend public school. Mom is willing to pay the entire bill for private school, but Dad thinks it's an attempt to show that he isn't paying his part. Mom explains that her father, who is now very ill, has set up a special fund to pay for Jake's education, including private school. Dad replies that while understands this is a generous gift from a grandparent, he is worried that Jake will know he's not paying toward it, and that makes him feel like an inadequate parent.

Dad drops Jake off in a new-to-him car. Mom is fuming because she feels that she doesn't receive enough financial support, but here he is with a new expensive item. The next time they are at one of Jake's soccer games, Mom makes a negative comment to Jake about Dad's new car.

In the first scenario, Mom and Dad need to take a step back to discuss that this decision is about the type of education they want to give their son, not where the money will come from. Mom can reduce the sense of judgment by reminding Dad that she's not paying either; the money is from a fund set up for this purpose. If the mutual answer is that private school is the best option, they can both tell Jake that he'll be attending private school without mentioning how it will be paid for. If he asks, they can agree to tell him that they only have his best education as their concern, and there is the money to pay for this.

In the second scenario, Dad reminds Mom that his father recently died, and it was left to him in his will. He had been close with his father, and he tells her the car reminds him each day of his father. He adds that it allows him to share an important part of his dad with Jake.

Reducing or removing judgments when discussing a sensitive subject will help both parents come to an understanding of the situation and aid in making a mutually agreeable resolution. Passing judgment without knowing the full story leads to unnecessary and unfounded angst within ourselves and with our co-parents.

K.

Kindness

When you go through a breakup, the last thing you want to do is be kind. You want your ex to know the hurt they caused. You want them to know how wrong you think they are. You want them to feel the same pain you do. These feelings often result in lashing out; sending texts full of anger, frustration, and blame, all of which mask your sadness. The pain keeps you stuck in time instead of moving forward. The lingering sadness and hurt not only harm you and your relationship with your ex, but the negative emotions also ultimately harm your kids. They feel your pain, no matter how much you try to hide it by crying in the bathroom or screaming in your car. They see you carry around these feelings of rejection and distress. Getting to a place where you can be kind to your ex, at least when it comes to your children, is best for everyone. If there is no other reason to show your ex kindness, remember that your children are watching and learning from you.

Examples

Mom needs minor surgery on her knee, which requires an overnight stay at the hospital, followed by a two-day stint at a physical rehabilitation facility, and then a few weeks of home rehab. Her mother will stay with her during this period, so Grandma will have plenty of time with Jake. Mom reaches out to Dad and offers to let Jake stay with him while she is in the hospital and at the physical rehab facility. She knows he'd really appreciate the extra time with their son.

Dad's mother needs his help moving from her house to an assisted living facility. This process has been emotionally difficult for Dad. Mom offers to take Jake for a few days while Dad is helping his mother. She then reassures Dad that they can schedule any missed time when Dad has settled his mother into her new abode. She also shares that she has a friend who recently went through this with her mother and offers to get the contact information for the social worker who spoke with her friend.

In the first case, Dad is thrilled to have Jake for a few extra days, and he is very touched that he was offered this option, especially because Mom didn't have to. In return for her kindness, he offers to bring Jake to see her in the hospital after her operation.

In the second case, Mom is not only showing kindness by allowing Dad the time he needs to move his mother but also offering to share useful information that could help with the emotional process.

When showing kindness, don't focus on the need balance every minute of time with your child. Instead, focus on how you can work together in a time of need. Over a period of years, time with your child will go back and forth as you and your ex make scheduling changes. The result is that the time usually sorts itself out in the end. Remember that kindness begets kindness and allows for a successful co-parenting relationship.

L.

Learn

Be willing to learn from your mistakes and to apologize when it's the right thing to do. When you let your ex know you're sorry for what you said or did, and you are sincere in your apology, it can go a long way toward repairing both old and new wounds. And remember, no one is a perfect parent. We all have our strengths and areas in which we can improve. Acknowledging that you are not always right makes you human; admitting that to yourself and your ex makes you a better co-parent. Part of protecting your child means protecting your child's relationship with the other parent. No parent-child relationship is perfect, but a child who has a supportive and healthy relationship with both parents is a child who grows into a more secure and compassionate adult.

Examples

At the beginning of the divorce, Mom sent Dad several angry and offensive texts. She was coming from a deeply hurt and emotional place. She and Dad were in a fragile part of the divorce process, when new schedules and communication processes were being created.

When Mom and Dad got divorced, Dad started dating right away. For months in a row, he introduced Jake to several women, even though none of the relationships became serious. Mom is not pleased about Dad's actions and the questions Jake was asking her about dating. As time went on, Dad realizes that introducing Jake to people he was not seriously interested in was confusing Jake about what it takes to form a real relationship.

As Mom came to terms with her role in the divorce, she feels terrible about the texts. She learned this was an overreaction and that she needs to apologize for what she said. Taking the time to communicate via email, she writes to Dad: "I wanted to tell you I am sorry I am for what I said when we first started the divorce process. I realize that some of the texts I sent were mean and hurtful, and I'm very sorry about my actions. It's my hope that, now that the ugliness of the divorce is over, we can work together for Jake's sake. I think we can be better co-parents than we were a married couple, and I'm willing to work toward that." Mom has learned an important lesson, and if Dad accepts her apology, their co-parenting will be stronger.

Dad learned his behavior was teaching Jake the wrong things about adult relationships. He reaches out to Mom via email: "It occurs to me that I made a mistake in introducing Jake to some of the women I have been dating. I should have waited until things were more settled, and until I was in a long-term, committed relationship. I have apologized to Jake, but also wanted to apologize to you."

M.

Mistakes

You will make mistakes, and so will your ex. No one is perfect and understanding and accepting that goes a long way toward successful co-parenting. There will be times when an argument will get heated or even out of control. It may be something you said, something your ex heard, or a misinterpretation of something texted. When it happens, take a step back. As I've advised throughout this book, take a breath. Don't text or call. Only communicate via email, and not until things calm down and you are in a better place emotionally. Why something goes off track is not as important as simply realizing that somewhere along the way someone (or both of you) made a co-parenting mistake. Co-parenting is a winding, not a linear, process. It may be two steps forward and five steps back. The most important lesson is to know when to hit pause and take a breath before you dig yourselves in more deeply and make bigger mistakes.

Examples

As Dad and Jake are on their way to school, Jake realizes that he left his homework folder on the kitchen table. Dad texts Mom to let her know and that he will tell the teacher. Mom has had a difficult morning already, and she sees this as another example of Dad not being a responsible parent. She replies, "If you can't get Jake ready for school appropriately, maybe we need to have Jake stay with me during the week." Dad is taken aback. They had a long, drawn-out custody battle and finally settled on the current schedule. He texts back, "Given how you are clearly not working on the anger issues that you've had for years, maybe we should go back to court so Jake can live with me full time." Mom is incensed. About to fire back at Dad, she recognizes that the feelings she's having, including flushed skin, tension in her back, and the headache coming on, are all a result of this interaction. And she's had them before.

Dad walks into Jake's basketball game and sees Mom with her boyfriend. Dad has thought for a while now that the boyfriend is trying to act like a father to Jake. Dad immediately walks out of the game and texts Mom from the parking lot, "I can't believe you would bring HIM to a basketball game when you knew I was going to be there. I would never do that to you but all you do is think about yourself and not anyone else. So typical of you." Mom texts back, "Why are you still upset about this? You and I are not together anymore. Why can't you accept that my boyfriend likes watching Jake's games?"

As you know by now, Mom needs to take a deep breath and realize from her body responses that she's made a mistake telling her ex he's not a good enough parent, and it's one she's made before. She replied with an overreaction to a text about a homework issue. She takes a few minutes to think about why she wrote what she did. Because there's no time to email, she texts back, "I'm sorry. I appreciate you letting me know about the homework folder. I have not had a good morning, but I should not have taken it out on you."

And in the second case, Dad walks around his car a few times. He knows he made a mistake—the boyfriend is a part of his ex's life, whether he likes it or not. He texts back, "I was surprised to see him there, and I overreacted. I did not mean to start a fight. I'm sorry about that. I'm coming back in."

N.

Normalcy

The process of breaking up is difficult for everyone—the co-parents and the children. The children are trying to figure out new family rules and where they are living on which days. Will they get to go to the same schools, will they have the same neighborhood friends, will they be involved in the same activities? Providing a sense of normalcy, as much as can be mustered through a tumultuous time, is vital. One way to do this with a co-parent is to write things down. Get a shared electronic calendar and notate who has which weekend, how the summer will be divided, who gets which holidays, and which days during those holidays. Agreeing and then setting it out in writing are the best ways to get on the same page and avoid any later misunderstandings. Prepare a calendar every six months or once a year, so planning is not a daily or monthly hassle. This allows both co-parents to start new lives and offers steadiness and certainty for the children.

Examples

Mom and Dad need to make joint decisions about Jake's schedule when he's out of school for the year, and they each get to choose a summertime activity to do with Jake. Dad wants to sign Jake up for golf lessons, but Mom wants to go to her family's summer cabin with Jake for two weeks at the start of the summer. This trip has become a ritual for her entire family. Both Mom and Dad want to schedule activities so they can prepare Jake for his summer, but there's a conflict with the timing of the two activities.

Jake's teacher reports that Jake is having a hard time with the divorce. Mom thinks it's Dad's fault because he is the one who asked for the divorce in the first place. Dad thinks it's Mom's fault because she hasn't moved on with her own life.

When it comes to Dad and Mom in the first example, they want to create some normalcy for Jake throughout the summer. They can reach a compromise if Dad offers to start Jake's golfing lessons after Mom's family camp trip. That way Jake isn't losing golfing instruction time or missing out on the trip. Finding an agreeable resolution together that benefits Jake, rather than having a judge decide, is a much more efficient way to co-parent and ultimately better for Jake.

For Mom and Dad in the second example, they need stop finding fault with each other and instead concentrate on the fact that Jake is having a hard time. They need to help him find some normalcy so he can make it through this stressful process. The wiser option is to discuss this together with the teacher and find out what is best for Jake. Might that mean sending him to a private counselor or having him meet with the school counselor? Would it include Mom and Dad each seeking help too, to learn how to co-parent? Giving Jake the foundation to process the family's transition will help him feel supported through an emotional time and find a semblance of normalcy in this new family dynamic.

O.

Others

When a new romantic partner is added to your family, it is tempting for that person to add their two cents to your parenting issues. Fight against that. Your significant other can act as your confidante, but they need to reign in their opinion of your ex as a person and a parent, especially when your children are around. Only you and your ex can determine what is best for your children. Remember that children can always overhear and overshare, even when you think they are not listening. Imagine how your ex would feel to hear negative comments from your new partner. Before that can happen, ask your new partner to work with you for the benefit of the children, and that can occasionally mean keeping some thoughts to themselves.

Examples

Mom's brother is in town for dinner on Sunday, but Dad is supposed to have Jake on Sundays. He can't stand Mom's brother because he has been rude to Dad's new wife at family functions. Mom has asked if she can take Jake on that one Sunday, since it is a special event. Dad's new wife is angry and asks why they would do any favor involving that brother.

*Dad and Mom can't even talk, text, or email each other without
including a barb or an insult about their new spouses. Jake has a
science project due on Monday. The project was started at Dad's
house, but Jake forgot it to pack it up. Now he's at Mom's house for
weekend. Dad's new wife is especially annoyed that they have to
spend part of this weekend fixing this problem.*

In the first case, Dad knows his wife is upset, and he can't blame
her. He also knows, however, that Mom's brother isn't in town
very often and that Jake loves his uncle. Dad can talk to his wife
while Jake is away from the house, and ask her to shift her focus
from the uncle to Jake. Thinking about what would be good for
Jake means stepping back from their opinion of the brother. One
alternative to help the situation would be to allow the switch in
scheduling but also ask for another day in exchange.

Since Jake is the one who forgot the project, and Jake's mom
brings him to school on Mondays, Dad's new wife thinks the
solution is for Jake's mother to come get it. Dad understands that
he didn't remember about the project either as he was getting
Jake's luggage and school backpack into the car. He comes up
with some ideas that he discusses with her. While she would still
prefer Jake's mom to come get the project, she agrees with him.
Dad sends a message to Mom, "Just checking in to see the best
way for me to get you the science project. Do you want me to
drop it off at your house this afternoon? Or would you rather
I bring it directly to school on Monday? Other thoughts? Let
me know what you think. Thanks." With Dad's new wife now
focused on resolving the issue in the way that's best for Jake, she
can let Jake's parents sort this out.

P.

Professionalism

It doesn't matter if you are not on friendly terms with your ex, you still need to act professionally toward them. You and your ex are in this parenting business together. You both need to act in the same way you would with someone you don't particularly like at your workplace. Your emails and texts should be cordial, respectful, not overly complicated, and not filled with emotion. You would not call a co-worker by a nasty name, chastise them, or belittle them. How you act at work is how you should act toward your ex. It's easier said than done, of course, but always using respectful communication will help during any encounters.

Examples

Dad asks to bring his girlfriend to the upcoming parent-teacher conference so she can hear what the teacher has to say about Jake's progress. After all, she's been in Jake's life for a long time. Mom is uncomfortable having her there because they used to be really close friends, and her presence will make it too hard for Mom to focus on what the teacher is saying.

Dad wants to switch weekends so he can take Jake on a vacation with his parents. Mom says no because she already has plans that weekend. Dad's first inclination is to immediately text Mom, "Once again, you put your own needs above Jake's. I don't know what your plans are, but why can't you stop being so petty and mean and start thinking about someone other than yourself?"

In the first case, Mom decides to send an email to Dad: "I know you want to bring your girlfriend to the parent-teacher conference, but since I am not yet comfortable with this situation, I would prefer she not attend. If you feel strongly that she come with you, let's do separate parent-teacher conferences this time and we can reassess next time." By keeping the emotion out of her message, offering a solution, and suggesting that the current situation may not always be the case, Mom has offered a professional compromise in a difficult situation.

In the second case, Dad realizes his response is not professional and won't help the situation. He instead emails, "I'm not sure what your plans are for the weekend, but this trip is to celebrate Granny's 90th birthday. My parents were hoping we would all spend it together, so if you would reconsider, I would appreciate it. I would be happy to switch weekends with you, either the weekend before or after, so that you are not losing time with Jake. Just let me know what might work for you. Thanks in advance."

These interactions are the kinds you would use at work when dealing with a difficult situation. Both parents are being professional as they work out changing plans, and the outcome will be more positive for everyone.

Q.

Question

Question why you are saying something, what you hope to achieve, and how your ex might interpret it. You and your ex may not be in the same place emotionally. Often, following a divorce, the person who initiated it is further along emotionally than the other partner. As you approach an issue, question yourself: Is it really a problem? Does something really need to be said? If so, what purpose does it serve? How can you say it so it's not misinterpreted?

Examples

Mom learns that Jake has been late to school the past two days. Mom texts Dad, "So I was told that Jake was late to school again today, just like he was yesterday. Is it impossible for you to get him to school on time?"

Dad sees that Mom has booked a pediatrician's appointment for Jake and put it on their shared calendar. Dad is mad because he can't make it, and once again, Mom failed to check the calendar before scheduling a medical appointment. Dad texts, "How many times do I have to tell you to check the calendar before you set an appointment for Jake to make sure I can attend? It's not going to happen anymore. I called and cancelled the appointment. Next time, check the calendar first before you schedule anything."

In the first instance, it would help if Mom remembered that she initiated the divorce, and Dad may be struggling to adjust to this new reality and new schedule. A better response would be to question why this keeps happening. Mom could text: "I got an alert that Jake was late to school today. Is everything ok? We know how he hates getting up early so, if there's anything I can do to help, just let me know." Helping to fix the problem rather that set the blame is far more beneficial for Jake.

In the second instance, Dad could question his own reaction and ask himself why Mom made the mistake again. He knows Mom used to make the medical appointments for Jake, and it didn't matter if she was the only parent there. This "forgetfulness" could be a sign that Mom is slower to make the transition to two households. A better option for Dad would be to respond: "I see that you made a pediatrician's appointment on July 1. On the calendar it's marked that I'm busy that day, so I called the doctor's office. They also have appointments on July 5 at 9:30 a.m., noon, and 2 p.m., and on July 6 at 11 a.m. and 4:15 p.m. Do any of these work for you? Let me know by tomorrow morning and I'll reschedule so we can both attend."

R.

Respond

A common phrase used in co-parenting is "respond, don't react." Allow yourself the space and the time to consider your options, weigh the possible outcomes, and then decide from a more neutral stance what to do next. It's hard, but stop yourself from doing something you will regret and can't undo. Take a pause before you say or do something you can't take back. When you give yourself the gift of time to take a breath and step away from your immediate response, you are helping yourself psychologically, helping your co-parenting relationship, and helping your child.

Examples

Mom and Jake are not getting along because he doesn't like the restrictions that Mom has set since he got his license, so he complains to Dad. Dad texts, "Jake tells me you are arguing about his driving privileges. It seems to me that Jake is a responsible kid, and we should trust him to do the right thing rather than try to control his behavior." Mom reads this and is outraged. She is being called controlling again, just like when they were married.

Dad lets six-year-old Jake ride on a tractor at his parents' farm over the weekend. Jake comes home and tells Mom all about driving the tractor. He is so excited! She is angry with Dad because it was crazy to let Jake drive. She texts Dad, "I can't believe you let Jake drive a tractor this weekend. How could you be so senseless? He's only 6 years old! He could have gotten seriously hurt!" Dad immediately gets angry that once again she is calling him an irresponsible father.

In the first instance, Mom wisely chooses to take a time out to consider her response. She decides to first reach out to another divorced mother who has always given her good advice. She helps Mom to understand Dad's text in another way: he thinks it's better to trust Jake now that he's becoming an adult rather than try control his actions like when he was younger. Mom now sees this as opportunity to come together for rules on Jake's driving, not as a condemnation of her parenting. She texts back, "Maybe it would be helpful for us and Jake if we are on the same page about restrictions on driving. I was thinking about an 11 p.m. curfew on weekends and no more than one other person in the car at a time. What do you think?"

In the second instance, Dad rereads her text before firing back a response. Why would she ever think he'd let Jake drive a tractor by himself? Then he remembers that Jake also told his grandparents at dinner that he'd "driven" the tractor. At dinner, that was funny, but he can see how hearing this out of context would make Mom so angry. He texts back, "I want you to know that Jake was with me the entire time. I did not let him out of my sight once, and when he says he 'drove the tractor,' it was really just him sitting with me with his hands on the wheel, but the tractor wasn't moving. I can understand why you misunderstood, but I hope you realize that I would never do anything to put Jake in harm's way."

S.

Silence

Not every contact needs a response. Few interactions need rehashing after they are over. It's so easy to want to have the last word, and it's so easy to get in one more thought or opinion with the speed of technology—but it is usually a bad idea. Reviewing a message and deciding whether it even needs a response is the first step in co-parenting communication. Often, it is best to not respond at all and just be silent from your end. Figure out whether you want to respond because you want to be "right" or because it's the right thing to do as a good co-parent. When you simply want to prove a point or show that the other person is wrong, you are coming from a defensive place and misplacing your focus on you and your relationship with your ex instead of on your child. When allowing your ego to get in the way and your emotions to take hold, you are giving in to a selfish impulse rather than stepping outside of the situation to look at what is best for your child. At this point, stop, allow room for silence, and take some time to center yourself. Is a response necessary? Will it help the situation? Or will it create more negative co-parenting interactions? Responding before thinking can create a series of events fueled by nothing more than hurt or anger. Communicating well with a co-parent means sharing important and necessary information. Poor communication includes saying something just because you want to.

Examples

Mom and Dad attend Jake's back-to-school night together. Dad was talking with the gym teacher about the school's new playground, so he missed the first few minutes of the homeroom teacher's introduction. Mom is livid. This is just like Dad to be more concerned about sports than about Jake's schooling.

Dad picks Jake up from school for his weekend. He sees that his son doesn't have his soccer ball, and he had specifically asked Mom to make sure Jake had the ball today. Mom knows that Dad and Jake play soccer together every weekend. Dad thinks this is another slight by Mom to try to ruin his time with Jake. Dad picks up his phone to angrily text Mom about this.

In the first scenario, Mom could say something, but what would it accomplish? Dad won't respond well to Mom chastising him, and he is likely only going to ignore her. Saying something will increase the bad feelings on both sides. When Mom allows some silence before her response, she realizes that, in this case, the introduction wasn't essential to hear. Mom may still have issues with Dad about Jake's schooling, but she realizes missing the introduction isn't worth making the situation worse.

In the second scenario, Dad could have easily texted Mom once again with a complaint. Or he could take a breath and allow room for silence where his anger had been. Dad decides in that silence that he and Jake can go buy a new soccer ball to keep at Dad's house. That way this particular battle never has to reoccur.

By staying silent and solving the problem productively, Dad's co-parenting relationship isn't made worse.

When deciding on how and when to communicate with your ex, realize that staying silent can be a good option.

T.

Time

When you need to respond to your ex about something important, keep time in mind. If your ex connected with you about an important issue, respond in a timely manner, as soon as you have the information and have a clear idea of the next step. Conversely, if you need a response that is time-sensitive, note that in your communication with your ex. And neither of you should wait until the last minute to ask for an immediate response because that will only create unnecessary problems. The more time you can give each other to think about the question or issue and respond back constructively, the better, especially if it's something that requires coordination between the two of you. If you receive an important message from your ex, consider all your options but respond in a time-sensitive manner.

Examples

Dad wants to take 10-year-old Jake to Mexico for a week in the summer with his new family (a trip he has scheduled at the last minute), but Jake does not have a passport. Because of Jake's age, both parents must apply for his passport, and there's now a rush to get that done.

Mom wants to sign Jake up for baseball in the spring. Jake already plays hockey in the winter, and the seasons overlap a little. Mom enjoys watching Jake play baseball more than hockey, which Dad knows. Mom asks Dad about signing Jake up for baseball because teams are forming over the next two weeks. Dad knows if he drags out his answer, Jake may not get on a baseball team, and that means Dad has more time to practice hockey with Jake through the summer.

The solution to the first case is that Dad needs to plan this trip with enough time so that he and Mom can first talk about the trip and then coordinate a time for them to get Jake's passport. Waiting to schedule the trip and then having to rush the passport process will only create unnecessary tension and conflict. If Dad reaches out to Mom, for example six months before the trip, she has the time respond within a few days or a week, and they can make plans that don't make either parent feel put out.

With the second case, Dad could delay his response long enough so that Jake misses the opportunity to try out for baseball. He also knows that if does that, Mom may not agree to let Jake playing hockey next winter. He takes the time to realize he would not want Mom to take advantage of him if their places were reversed. The next day, he texts Mom that he's in agreement with letting Jake try out for baseball.

U.

Unintentional

When you think about the actions of your ex who hurt you, it is easy to misinterpret what they do through the lens of hurt and anger. However, unless you are in a truly unhealthy relationship with your ex (and again, that is beyond the scope of this book), it is more likely that your ex's actions weren't done specifically to hurt you, and any ill-effects were unintentional. How often have you said or done something only to learn later you created unintentional pain? It's easy to lash out right away, but it's important to take a step back to reevaluate the situation.

Examples

Jake is telling Mom about his week with Dad, including that Dad's new girlfriend slept over on Friday night. Mom is irate. She knows Dad is dating, but letting new his girlfriend spend the night while Jake is there is too much. Mom fires off a text: "I can't believe you let someone you've just started dating stay over at your house when you have Jake. We fought in court because you wanted equal time with Jake, but here you are spending your time with our son and with someone else. What were you thinking?"

Jake tells Dad that Mom and Uncle John took him around town to take some pictures. Jake wants to submit one of those pictures to the yearbook. Dad is upset because he wanted to be a part of having Jake's senior pictures taken. Dad sees this as yet another example of Mom keeping him out of Jake's important events. He texts, "I told you I wanted to be there for Jake's senior pictures, and he just told me that you already got them done. Why didn't you let me know this was happening? I shouldn't have to hear about this from Jake. Stop trying to push me out of his life!" Mom quickly types, "I never pushed you out of his life. You never wanted to get involved! Now all of a sudden you want to be super-dad, but we know that's far from the truth. The photos are not the official pictures, it was just something my brother wanted to try out as a new hobby. Stop trying to always make me look like a bad person!"

In the first example, Dad writes an angry text, but before he sends it, he puts down his phone to take a breath. He realizes this is going to spiral out of control and get them nowhere. He erases the text and sends instead, "I did not intend for her to stay over on Friday. I've not had girlfriends stay over while I have Jake with me, but she had an asthma attack and couldn't drive home. She stayed on the couch and I explained to Jake why she was staying over. He just didn't explain it all to you. Please let me know if you have any other questions."

In the second example, Mom doesn't send her text either. She knows this will get them nowhere and is just a recycling of old arguments. She instead texts, "The photos were just pictures taken by my brother as a new hobby, they are not the official pictures. I know it's important for both of us to be there for the studio pictures. I will make sure we schedule that together and jointly decide which one to use."

V.

Vortex

It's easy to find yourself in a vortex of emotions when you are co-parenting. The actions or words of your ex may bring up memories and feelings from a long time ago. Or not so long ago, too. In those moments, you may find yourself lost, angry, confused, hurt, and sad; and it's easy to want to lash out. Don't. The vortex of emotions you are feeling will pass. Realize that your relationship with your ex is in the past. While it was significantly painful to go through the divorce, you are now in a place where you should focus on your future. Talk to a friend (but see D. Discretion). Engage a therapist. Don't let these negative thoughts rule you and undo all the work you've done to be a good co-parent. Do the work to stay on track and prevent yourself from being derailed again by a vortex of emotions.

Examples

Mom is getting remarried only seven months after divorcing Dad, who is devastated because she is marrying the man she had an affair with during the marriage. Mom obviously wants Jake to attend her wedding. Dad bribes Jake that he'll take him to Disneyworld for the weekend of the wedding. Jake realizes he'll have to choose between his parents, and Mom is furious that Jake might miss her wedding.

Mom can't pick up Jake from school and take him to his base-ball game because of a change in her work schedule. She asks her boyfriend to help out. Dad is the coach of the baseball team, and he sees this substitution as Mom shirking her parental duties. He is also infuriated that another man brought his son to practice when Dad could have picked Jake up and brought him to the game. He sends her an angry text that isn't nice about her or her boyfriend.

The first case is simply bad parenting because Dad didn't first process his feelings, but instead created a mess by acting while still in the vortex of his anger. He needs to deal with his anger and rejection with the help of a therapist. He did exactly what you don't want to do when co-parenting: he put Jake in the middle of an impossible situation.

The father's reaction in the second case may be more understandable, but it was still made in a vortex of anger. Mom couldn't control her work schedule, and she chose one way to get Jake to the game on time. She was doing her best to meet her parental duty to get their son safely to the game and on time. It is her prerogative to ask her boyfriend and not her ex for this favor. If he'd stopped to think first, he wouldn't have sent the message he can't take back.

W.

Work

Like any relationship, co-parenting takes work. It entails choosing your battles and letting other things go. It requires deciding when to speak up and when to not respond. Co-parenting is often uncomfortable because your once loving relationship with your ex has morphed into something different. It's not a new relationship because you already really know each other (you have a child together!), but you can't relate in the same way because that marriage structure is gone. Co-parenting involves work on both sides, not just one person doing the tough stuff and one showing up for the fun. Working together means each sharing and listening to what you think is best for your child. This is where the real work comes in, but it is the foundation of good co-parenting. Pay attention to what is going on at the other house when it's shared with you. This may require you working together so the important things are the same (or mostly the same) at both homes. Talk with each other and listen to what may be difficult to hear. It's all part of the work that is essential for you to co-parent effectively.

Examples
Mom tells Dad that Jake is acting out at her house. He's throwing temper tantrums after transitions back from Dad's house and he

isn't following rules, like putting his clothes away or making his bed each morning.

Dad got a new job and is planning to move closer to his office, which is in a new school district. When Mom and Dad first got divorced, they agreed to stay in the same district so Jake could ride the bus to school from either house. Dad is nervous about telling Mom and about upsetting Jake, but this new job will allow him to provide a better life for Jake and it's a big step in his career.

In the first scenario, it would be easy for Dad to think that Mom is doing something wrong, but instead he asks what's going on. Mom doesn't know. Dad offers to talk to Jake about following the rules at both houses. Mom suggests that Dad ask Jake if there is anything he wants to talk to about and then encourage him to do so. It turns out Jake simply doesn't like going over to Mom's at 7 p.m. on Sundays because he feels rushed. Mom and Dad discuss changing the time of transition. By listening to Mom's concerns, Dad was able to work with her to figure out what's going on with Jake. Together they changed the schedule to one that was better for Jake and helped make a better dynamic between Mom and Jake.

In the second scenario, Dad plunges in, open and direct, to tell Mom about his job and his move to a new house (and school district). She is initially quite upset. But the discussion reveals Dad isn't moving right away, so they can work together to make the best plan for Jake. They agree that Dad will drive Jake to and from school on his days, and Jake can keep taking the bus when he's with Mom. They then talk to Jake together about the new plans. With school transportation now worked out, she recognizes what a tremendous opportunity this is for her ex.

X.

eXpectations

These need to be realistic on both sides. There are stories of parents who got divorced but they still go away on vacation together with their children. While that's not a myth, it is significantly unrealistic for the majority of families. If you don't go on vacation together, host birthday parties together, or celebrate holidays together, it doesn't mean you hate each other, and it doesn't mean you're not good co-parents. You may sit together at sporting events, or you may attend recitals on different sides of the stage. Either way, "family together" time can simply be public events where the focus is on your child, or it can be a jointly hosted event. Remember, you are in the business of co-parenting, which does not mean being best friends. Set achievable expectations: get along cordially, think of your child first, and make things as comfortable for everyone as possible. Keeping those expectations appropriate will lead you to a good co-parenting relationship. It doesn't have to be perfect—it just has to work for your family and your child.

Examples

Mom is planning a sixth birthday party for Jake. She and Dad got divorced a little less than a year ago, and she thinks Jake seeing his parents together for his birthday might help him feel better about the divorce. Mom invites Dad, who says he would like to attend with his girlfriend. While Mom has known about the girlfriend, she certainly doesn't want to meet her for the first time at Jake's party. Mom says that she isn't uncomfortable with the idea. If Dad insists on his girlfriend attending, then Mom and Dad will have to have separate parties for Jake.

Jake has a soccer tournament out of town on Dad's time. Mom and Dad still are not getting along after the divorce, and being around each other remains tense and difficult both for them and Jake. They know that being at the same tournament for an entire weekend can make Jake uncomfortable. Nevertheless, Mom loves watching Jake play and to cheer him on.

Dad has a choice in the first example to attend Jake's birthday party by himself or hold a separate one with his girlfriend. He realizes that neither choice is wrong, but he has to consider which is better for Jake. His expectation was that he could attend with his girlfriend, but that was not correct.

Mom's expectation in the second example was that she'd attend the tournament out of town, but she recognizes that it's not a good idea for Jake right now. It would be too much stress for everyone. Mom tells Jake that she has a work event that weekend, but she knows Jake and Dad are going to have a great time together. She promises that she'll check in with him each day. Mom choosing to say she has to work over the weekend keeps Jake kept out of the middle and allows him to enjoy his tournament.

Y.

Yes

Say yes more often than you say no. If you assume that your ex is coming from a place of wanting the best for your child, just as you are, it changes your reaction when a request is made. Say yes to a special event that your child can attend with your ex. Say yes if your ex wants to go to therapy with your child to work on their relationship. Say yes to things that encourage your child to have a good relationship with the other parent. Children who have a bonded relationship with both parents grow up to be more fulfilled and well-rounded adults. Any therapist will tell you that the "Mommy" issues and "Daddy" issues that we struggle with as adults are born in our childhoods. Having a good, or even passable, relationship with both parents helps a child in the long run.

Examples
There is a mother-son dance for Jake's seventh-grade class on one of Dad's nights. Mom wants to take Jake to the dance, buy him a suit, and go out for a special dinner the night of the dance.

Jake's high school graduation is coming up. Jake is scheduled to be with Dad the night before and all day after the graduation. Mom's family is coming in from out of town the evening before the graduation. Mom asks if Jake can come to her house the night before graduation to have dinner with her family. She promises that Jake will be home by 10 p.m. and reminds Dad that he'll still have the entire day after graduation with Jake.

In the first case, if Dad assumes Mom is doing this to strengthen her relationship with Jake and to make special memories, then there's no reason not to say yes. If instead Dad assumes that Mom is doing this only to take time away from him, he would say no. When they talk over the phone and Dad hears how excited Mom is, the answer for Dad is clear. Of course it's about Jake and not about his ex "doing" something to take away time from him.

In the second case, Dad needs to think about Jake spending time with both sides of his extended family for his graduation. The answer is obviously yes, because this event is just as important for him as for Mom. If Dad only thinks in terms of Mom trying to usurp time with Jake, which is self-centered thinking, his answer would be no. By putting the focus on everyone's anticipation of the graduation and that it's best for Jake to share this important time, the answer is clearly yes.

Z.

Zealous

Zealously guard your co-parenting relationship. There will be people who try to get in the way. They may not mean to, but they will. The most important thing you can do for your child is to be a good co-parent with your ex. Friends and family, even significant others, may share their opinions about what you and your ex should or shouldn't do. Those voices don't really matter when you and your ex work together for what is best for your child. People will offer advice. Maybe it'll be worthwhile, but if it doesn't work for you and your ex and your child, ignore it. It is your job to zealously remember that co-parenting is about working with your ex and focusing on your child. Make that relationship untouchable and immovable. There are no set rules for co-parenting. There is no checklist that will tell you how to raise your child. There is a lot of guidance and advice offered by friends, family, and websites. There is this book by a divorce attorney and a divorced co-parent. But in the end, it's you deciding with you ex on what is best for your child living in two houses.

Examples
Dad's mother wants to take Jake shopping for school clothes. Dad knows that Mom always takes Jake shopping for school clothes and makes a special day of it. Dad's mother berates Dad about how he

should not be giving in to Mom all of the time. How can he zealously protect what he knows is a special time with his son and his ex, yet make his mother happy?

Mom's family have always been competitive swimmers, and Mom even went to college on a swimming scholarship. Jake likes to swim, but he prefers playing baseball, which is something that Dad's family has always done. Mom's parents and sibling continue to ask her why she doesn't stand up to Dad and insist that Jake make swimming more important.

In both cases, there are outside forces telling the co-parents what to do, when it not their place and their advice is not constructive.

Dad reaches out to Mom and lets her know that his mother would like to take Jake clothes shopping. He adds that he knows it's always been a special day for Mom and Jake. He asks if Mom would agree to let his mother buy Jake new sneakers and a winter coat. If Mom agrees to this compromise, Grandma gets to do some school shopping while Mom still gets to do the rest. Dad is zealously working to not intrude on Mom's back-to-school tradition with Jake. When Mom realizes Dad is trying his best in an uncomfortable family situation, she tells Dad that her ex-mother-in-law can do some shopping. Dad says he will make it clear to his mother she can buy only those two items.

Mom understands how important swimming is in her family but also recognizes that Jake doesn't like it as much as baseball. While it may be disappointing, there's nothing wrong that. Regardless of what her family thinks, Mom zealously guards Jake's needs and the relationship between her son and his father.

Conclusion

This book has been a guide on being divorced while effectively co-parenting a child. A good co-parenting relationship allows you to set aside your past relationship with your ex to focus on your child. It means taking the emotions out of your interactions with your ex. It means dealing with each other professionally and clearly as to how to raise your child to be the best adult possible. It's navigating new territory as a divorced couple yet remaining on course for raising your child. In the beginning, it is a real challenge. You may instead be focused on why the marriage didn't work out. What happened? You may experience anger or despair. You may feel scared and overwhelmed. This is when it's important to breathe, not respond too quickly or harshly, and to focus on constructive communication with your ex. Every child wants their parents to get along. Every child needs and deserves to know they are loved, even if their parents no longer love each other. Figuring out the best way forward for your child and working with your ex are vital goals after divorce. Working on, nurturing, and maintaining a good co-parenting relationship benefits everyone in the end.

Acknowledgments

This book, as with most, was a process of learning the material over many years and learning how to publish in a short time. I am grateful to all of my friends and mentors who have guided me along the way. Thank you to E and J for being my first readers and editors. Thank you to Lila for your guidance and thoughts. Thank you to Gloria and to Peggy for walking me through this each step of the way. As always, thank you to my children, my boyfriend, and my family. Thank you, as well, to my ex-husband, as we learned how to co-parent together.

Made in the USA
Monee, IL
14 May 2021